ISBN 978-0-260-48306-5
PIBN 11123668

1 MONTH OF
FREE
READING

at
www.ForgottenBooks.com

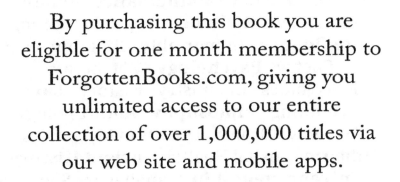

By purchasing this book you are eligible for one month membership to ForgottenBooks.com, giving you unlimited access to our entire collection of over 1,000,000 titles via our web site and mobile apps.

To claim your free month visit: www.forgottenbooks.com/free1123668

Historic, archived document

Do not assume content reflects current
scientific knowledge, policies, or practices.

PUPATION SITES OF PINK BOLLWORMS:
POTENTIAL MORTALITY RESULTING FROM
CULTIVATION OF IRRIGATED COTTON

ARS W-32
December 1975

WESTERN REGION

AGRICULTURAL RESEARCH SERVICE • U.S. DEPARTMENT OF AGRICULTURE

ABSTRACT

:ermine potential pupation sites of the pink boll-
lla (Saunders), and the mortality to be expected from
:tonfields. Tests indicate that pink bollworms tend
/ lumpy soil in which some trash has accumulated,
(32° to 37° Celsius), and somewhat damp (less than 20
leal conditions, which exist in the part of the row
, become even more favorable as the plant canopy
s decrease, cultivation ceases, and more trash accum-
survival contributes to larger, more damaging, late-
)ollworms.

, Cultivation, Insects, Irrigation, Light,
:e, Pink bollworm, Mortality, Pressure,
)n, Soil textures, Temperature.

CONTENTS

:icultural Research Service
'TATES DEPARTMENT OF AGRICULTURE
    In Cooperation With
Agricultural Experiment Station

PUPATION SITES OF PINK BOLLWORMS: POTENTIAL MORTALITY
RESULTING FROM CULTIVATION OF IRRIGATED COTTON

By R. E. Fye[1] and H. L. Brewer[2]

INTRODUCTION

During the analysis of insect populations in the field, in which the pupating individuals bury themselves in the soil, the population analyst must con-
sider the potential mortality among these individuals due to the normal cultivation of the field. The following studies were made to determine the potential
pupation sites of the pink bollworm, *Pectinophora gossypiella* (Saunders), and
the mortality to be expected from cultivation of irrigated cottonfields.

METHODS AND MATERIALS

Pupation Site Preferences

Soil condition.--A test was conducted in the greenhouse to determine the
preferences of the pink bollworm for pupation sites in dried, irrigated soil
with cracks as compared with sites in cultivated soil, which were simulated by
passing the soil through a 6-mm mesh screen. The irrigated, cracked soil and
the loose soil were contained in plastic sweater boxes, 27 by 34.5 by 9 cm, and
presented to mature larvae as four paired containers taped together within a
plywood arena 30 cm deep. A bridge of loose soil, 50 mm wide, over the mutual
juncture allowed the pink bollworms access to either the cracked soil or the
cultivated soil. In an additional pair of boxes, only the irrigated, cracked
soil was offered in a similar plywood arena. The mature pink bollworm larvae
were introduced by suspending above the arena a 3.781-liter paper carton in
which the larvae had attained the prepupal stage. The mature larvae were allowed
to exit from the containers, which were suspended over the arenas for 30 hours.
At the end of 5 days, the cultivated soil was screened and the location of the
pupae determined. The various cracks and irregularities in the dry, irrigated soil were in-
spected to determine the location of the pupae in the dry, irrigated soil.

Soil surface.--The pupation site preferences of pink bollworms were studied
in arenas measuring 40 by 60 cm. The arenas were divided into six compartments
by 20- by 20-cm trays. Five of the compartments were filled to a depth of 6.5
cm with soil that had been sieved through a 6-mm screen. In the sixth compartment, which was 15 cm deep, three cracks--1.5, 2.5, and 3.5 mm wide--were cre-
ated by facing plywood blocks with a glue and soil mixture. The six trays form-
ing the compartments were then placed within the arena and covered with about 1
cm of sifted soil. One 20- by 20-cm area was left without any additional pupation site. Two 20- by 20-cm areas were covered with clods of soil, one with

[1]Research entomologist, Cotton Insects Biological Control Laboratory, Agricultural Research Service, 2000 E. Allen Road, Tucson, Ariz. 85719.

[2]Agricultural engineer, USDA-ARS-Southern Region, Grassland-Forage Research
Center, P.O. Box 748, Temple, Tex. 76501.

clods less than 1.5 cm in diameter and one with clods 1.5 to 3.5 cm in diameter. The two remaining trays were covered with loose layers of cotton leaves approximately 7 to 10 mm deep. One of the groups of leaves was mixed with sifted soil to simulate the situation commonly found immediately under cotton plants in the cotton rows. The other leaves were left loose on the surface of the soil. Cartons of reared pink bollworm larvae (6)[3] were placed over the three arenas, and the pink bollworms exiting from the cartons were allowed to pupate in the site of their choice in the three arenas. About 10 days later, each compartment was examined to determine where the pink bollworms had pupated.

Temperature.--A hexagonal arena, 60 cm on a side and 30 cm deep, was constructed to determine the temperature preferences of prepupae moving toward pupation sites. The hexagon was divided into six triangular sections, and a heating cable was installed in each of the sections. Ridges of sheet metal, 2.5 cm wide and 3.8 cm deep, separated the various sections and supported a covering of 6-mm hardware cloth cut to fit the interior of the arena. A layer of heavy aluminum foil was placed over the hardware cloth and taped to the edges of the arena so the heating cables for the heating chambers were sealed from the larvae placed in the arena. Strips of metal, 1.25 by 2.5 cm, were placed on the surface of the aluminum foil to separate the six sections of the arena. The arena was then filled to a depth of 1.25 cm with blown mica insulation. The thermostats controlling the heating cables were placed on the surface of the mica fill and then adjusted to the desired temperatures. Mature pink bollworm larvae exiting from rearing cartons (6) were introduced by allowing them to drop on a hexagonal platform in the center of the arena, which rested on the surface of the mica. Thus, the larvae were offered pupation sites with six choices of temperature. The test was conducted in total darkness so that light did not influence the preferences of the prepupae. After 5 days, the mica fill from each compartment was removed and sifted to determine the numbers of pink bollworms that had pupated in each temperature regimen.

Soil moisture.--A greenhouse test was run to determine the moisture preferences of the pink bollworm prepupae. Four 17- by 31-cm plastic shoeboxes were filled with clay loam soil and soaked from the bottom to various levels of moisture. At the start of the introductions, the untreated soil moisture in the four replicates ranged from 2 to 30 percent, and the soil in the three treatments ranged from 7 to 10 percent, 14 to 19 percent, and 25 to 27 percent of the dry weight of the soil. During the introduction of the pink bollworms, over a 48-hour period, the moisture loss was from 2 to 4 percent in the moistened soils. For the introduction, one replication of each soil treatment was placed in rectangular configuration within a plywood wall 30 cm deep. Cartons of pink bollworm larvae (6) that had reached the "cutout" stage were placed above the soil, and the larvae were allowed to select the soil with the moisture level of their preference. Three strips of cardboard, 2.5 by 28 cm, were placed on the surface of each box of soil and weighted to create a space into which the pink bollworms could enter and pupate. At the end of 5 days, the soil was sifted and examined to determine the location of the pupae.

Mortality

Burial.--Pink bollworm pupae in cocoons were buried at depths of 2.5, 5, 7.5, and 10 cm in finely sifted soil to determine from what depth the emerging adults could successfully emerge. Three centimeters of sifted soil were placed

---

[3]Italic numbers in parentheses refer to Literature Cited, p. 10.

in the bottom of a 1.9-liter ice cream carton with a diamter of 11 cm. Five replicates of 30 pupae were placed on the surface of the bottom soil and then buried to the desired depths with additional soil. The tests were conducted in the greenhouse with temperatures ranging from $20°$ to $38°$ Celsius in sandy loam and clay loam soils. After the adults had completely emerged, they were counted and the wing deformities noted.

Pressure.--In a preliminary test to determine the pressure necessary to kill pink bollworm pupae, four replicates of five naked pupae were subjected to pressures of 0.07, 0.35, and 0.70 kg/cm^2 for 0, 1, and 5 sec. The test was conducted in two types of soil, sandy loam and clay. The pupae were left on the soil surface and also buried 1.5, 2.5, and 10 cm in the soil before the pressures were applied. Two weeks later, the cans containing the soil and pupae were examined for the emergence of adult pink bollworms.

For the laboratory study of the potential mortality of pink bollworm pupae subjected to tillage pressure in the cracks in the soil, small clay blocks were made with thick clay slurry to simulate soil cracks in the field. Molds (10 by 15 by 5 cm) were first half filled, then a divider was inserted on which insect screening had been stapled on both sides to create a rough surface. After the divider was installed, an additional 5-cm layer of clay was poured into the mold, and the final mold side was put in place. When the clay was dry, the center divider was removed.

For the test, 25 5-day-old pink bollworm pupae in their cocoons were placed on the surface of the interior block of clay held in a horizontal position. Small slats, 5 mm thick, were inserted at the edge to hold the crack at that width as the outer clay block was put in place. The outside part of the form was then added, the protective slats removed, and the pressures applied to the outside of the form with a spring pressure gage (fig. 1). Pressures of 0.175, 0.35, 0.525, 0.70, and 0.875 kg/cm^2 were applied to each of four replicates. After the pressure had been applied, the crack was restored to the 5-mm width, and the molds with the treated pupae were held in ventilated plastic shoeboxes in a greenhouse in which early summer days were simulated with a daylight-to-dark photoperiod of 14:10 hr and daily temperatures ranging from $22°$ to $35°$ C. At the end of 21 days, the moths emerging from the treated pupae were counted.

Figure 1.--Pressure being applied with a pressure gage to pink bollworm pupae inserted between two small clay blocks.

Cultivation Pressures

The pressures expected through a normal cultivation of c
mined with specially developed capsules in a clay loam soil.
medicinal capsules (size No. 5) were wrapped twice with alumi
each 32 μ thick, forced closely against the interior wall of
part of the capsule. The capsules were calibrated by applyin
to the capsule with a pressure gage. The diameter of the con
then measured with a vernier caliper, and a regression of the
the pressure applied was developed.

In the field, the capsules were placed over the entire p
cotton row in various situations in which pink bollworms woul
pupate. The capsules were placed in small groups, and a stri
tic engineers' tape was placed near each group. The test are
vated with commonly used tillage equipment, consisting of two
cutting the soil away from the row, followed by 25-cm sweeps
disks to cultivate the side of the row, and, finally, a 37-cm
the proper level and configuration. After cultivation, the t
and the soil in the vicinity of the misplaced tapes was sifte
thoroughly to detect the capsules. The recovered capsules we
the thickness of the compressed foil within the capsules was
sion to determine the pressures that had developed within the

RESULTS AND DISCUSSION

Pupation Sites

The laboratory simulations of pupation sites of pink bol
the observations of entomologists associated with the pink bo
years. When given a choice, the pink bollworm prepupae show
for loose, cultivated soil rather than the cracks in recently
(table 1). The prepupae also seemed to prefer to remain in t
strata of the soil.

When confronted with a situation in which the soil is ge
and cracked, the pink bollworms seek out the small irregulari
surface and pupate there in preference to the deeper cracks;
penetrate into cracks (table 2) that are generally less than
of the soil of various sizes are added, a few will pupate und
most pink bollworms prefer the soil surface (table 2). If th
ered with leaves or other trash, a few will pupate within the
the trash; however, if the trash is incorporated into the soi
bollworms prefer the interface between the trash and the soil
tion site. Orphanides et al. (5), citing unpublished data of
the University of California, Riverside, noted that 50 percen
worms in the field select trash or debris in which to pupate.
bollworms penetrate into the soil, but the great majority rem
strata.

Overall, the irregularities in loose soil surfaces are p
tion sites; if trash is incorporated with these irregularitie
pink bollworms will pupate in these sites. During the tests,
would enter into the first irregularity and pupate if the soi
not too high. However, if the soil surface was overheated, t
sought a cooler site. They also sought areas with low light

4

Preliminary tests of the temperature preference of the mature pink bollworm larvae indicated that at approximately 38° C the response to temperature became negative. In the subsequent tests with temperatures above and below 38°, 41 percent of 266 pink bollworms preferred a pupation site at a temperature of 32°, 21 percent preferred a substrate at 34°, 31 percent entered the compartment held at 37°, but only 5 and 2 percent selected the compartments held at 39° or 44°, respectively. No pink bollworm prepupae entered the compartment held at a temperature of 49°. Because a constant temperature could not be maintained over the entire surface of the vermiculite, the prepupae entering the compartment held at 44 probably pupated in a cooler location.

In a subsequent test involving 219 prepupae, 50 percent entered a compartment held at 32° C, 23 percent and 21 percent entered two compartments held at 37°, and 6 percent entered a compartment held at 45°, but no prepupae entered two compartments held at 49°. The data confirmed that mature larvae are very sensitive to temperature and respond negatively when temperatures exceed 38°. Therefore, much of the cotton row profile early in the season (3) would not be an attractive site for the pupation of the pink bollworm due to the lack of shade, high soil temperatures, and excessive light.

As seen in table 3, moisture generally helps pink bollworms survive during pupation (2). There was no difference in the response of the pink bollworms to

Table 1.--*Pupation of pink bollworms in simulated cultivated and cracked soil*

Depth (cm)	Percentage of pink bollworms pupating in indicated sites					
	Cultivated soil	Cracks along side of container	Cracks in middle of container			
		7.0 mm wide	7.0 mm wide	3.5 mm wide	2.5 mm wide	Total
	Larvae offered choice of soils					
Surface	65.6					
Surface-1.25	10.9	3.7		0.7	2.4	6.8
1.26-3.75		2.0	0.5	1.0	1.7	5.2
3.76-6.25	[1]5.0	2.1	1.4	.3	.7	4.5
6.26-8.75		1.3	.5		.2	2.0
Total	81.5	9.1	2.4	2.0	5.0	18.5
	Larvae offered only cracked soil[2]					
Surface	[3]54.5					
Surface-2.5		7.4		8.0	14.8	30.2
2.6-3.75		3.1	1.8	1.8	3.7	10.4
3.76-5.00		3.1	.6		1.2	4.9
Total	54.5	13.6	2.4	9.8	19.7	45.5

[1]Includes all pupae deeper than 1.25 cm.
[2]Except loose soil bridge between containers.
[3]In soil in center of container.

Table 2.--*Pupation of 2,450 pink bollworms with a choice of pupation sites added to bare soil*

Choice	Percentage of pupae in--			
	Added sites	Soil surface[1]	Subsoil	Total
				Percent
Bare soil only		6.6	1.0	7.6
Bare soil vs. cracks		1.4		4.5
1.5-mm cracks	0.6			
2.5-mm cracks	1.0			
3.5-mm cracks	1.5			
Bare soil vs. clods <1.25 cm	1.2	5.8	2.5	9.5
Bare soil vs. clods 1.25 to 2.5 cm	5.5	12.2	3.2	20.9
Bare soil with surface trash	2.5	18.1	2.5	23.1
Bare soil with surface trash partially buried	10.3	[2]22.3	1.8	34.4
Total	22.6	66.4	11.0	100.0

[1] Top 9 mm.
[2] Includes soil in trash.

Table 3.--*Percentage of pink bollworms pupating by choice in several moisture regimes and pupation sites*

Item	Percentage of soil moisture			
	1.9-3.3	7.1-10.4	13.6-19.6	25.0-27.3
Insects pupating in moisture regime:				
Number	793	664	609	325
Percent	33.6	28.1	23.6	14.7
Percentage of pupae:				
Under strips and tapes[1]	21.3	27.7	22.1	67.0
In top 1.25 cm of soil	55.4	62.0	74.8	33.0
Deeper than 1.25 cm in soil	23.2	10.2	2.9	0

[1] Provided a loose interface with soil surface.

the several moisture regimens until the moisture level exceeded 20 percent. At the higher level, the pink bollworms used the added strips and tapes for pupation sites and only a small percentage pupated in the excessively moist soil. Therefore, moisture probably would not be a major factor in the selection of a pupation site during most of the season in irrigated areas although it would influence soil temperatures. However, the decreased response of pink bollworms to soils with more than 20 percent moisture indicates that recently irrigated soil would not be selected as a pupation site unless no other sites were available. Because the portion of the bed directly under the plants has a lower water content during irrigation than the remainder of the row profile, the pink bollworm would have adequate pupation sites that were suitable during a major irrigation or rainy period.

In the three lower moisture regimes, pupation occurred mostly in the top 1.25 cm of soil. As the soil moisture increased, the prepupae did not penetrate as deeply into the soil. Similar numbers pupated in the three lower moisture regimens under the strips of cardboard placed on the surface to simulate trash. In the very wet soil, the majority of the pink bollworms pupated under the strips and under the tapes along the edge of the box. Some pupated in the soft, irregular parts of the top 1.25 cm of the soil. However, no pink bollworms penetrated the extra moist soil below the surface.

The ideal pink bollworm pupation site, then, is a loose, slightly lumpy soil surface in which some trash is accumulated, shaded to be cool and dark, and somewhat damp. The part of the row profile directly under the cotton plants meets all the criteria: It has loose soil containing spent petals and fallen leaves, proper shade, a drier area during irrigation, and the longest period of moisture retention as the soil dries after irrigation or rain.

Cultivation

Normal cotton cultivation generally breaks the soil surface to depths of only 5 to 8 cm to avoid excessive root pruning. The disks that cut to the depth of the cultivated layer along each side of the row leave a band of undisturbed soil from 15 to 18 cm wide. Thus, approximately 15 percent of the total row area and a much higher percentage of the ideal pupation refuge of the pink bollworm are left undisturbed.

Because the tillage is relatively shallow (5 to 8 cm), the mortality due to burial alone in the area that is disturbed might range from 33 to 90 percent (table 4). The data indicate the mortality may be somewhat higher in the sandy soils, possibly due to increased abrasion and attending desiccation.

The preliminary study of the pressures required to kill pink bollworms (table 5) indicated that when a pressure of 0.07 kg/cm^2 was applied to open, naked pupae and pupae buried 1.25 and 2.5 cm below the surface a low percentage were killed. However, when pressures of 0.35 kg/cm^2 were applied, as many as 45 percent of the pupae were killed, and when pressures of 0.70 kg/cm^2 were

Table 4.--*Mortality of pink bollworm moths emerging from pupae buried in sifted clay and sandy loam soils*

Burial depth (cm)	Mortality[1]		Deformed wings[2]		Effective emergence[3] [4]	
	Clay	Sandy loam	Clay	Sandy loam	Clay	Sandy loam
	----------------------------------Percent----------------------------------					
0	20	44	0	0		
2.5	54	66	4	4	67	61
5.0	71	83	14	30	36	30
7.5	81	94	37	50	24	11
10.0	92	97	57	85	10	5

[1]150 pupae buried at each depth in each soil type.

[2]Percentage based on number emerged.

[3]Corrected with Abbott's (1) formula for mortality in check, that is, 20 percent in clay and 44 percent in sandy loam soils.

[4]Normal functional moths.

Table 5.--*Mortality of pink bollworm pupae after applying 3 levels of pressure for 1 or 5 seconds to each of 20 pupae in 2 soil types*

Depth of pupae in soil (cm)	Number of seconds pressure applied	Pupal mortality after applying the following pressures, in kg/cm^2, to--							
		Sandy loam soil				Clay			
		0	0.07	0.35	0.70	0	0.07	0.35	0.70
		------Number dead------							
0	0	2				4			
	1		1	2	13		1	2	9
	5		1	2	17		0	5	8
1.25	0	3				2			
	1		2	6	20		5	4	18
	5		2	3	20		2	9	17
2.5	0	1				1			
	1		2	8	17		5	4	11
	5		1	4	19		0	7	15

applied, 100 percent of the pupae buried 1.25 cm in the sandy soil were killed. In most cases, extending pressure by 5 seconds did not increase the mortality. Generally, when the pressure was applied to the sandy loam soil, the mortality was greater than in the clay soils. The data again suggest that the abrasiveness of the sand granules may have resulted in a greater desiccation of the treated pupae in the sand than in the clay.

The more extensive study, summarized in table 6, indicated that the mortality due to pressure was quite variable but increased greatly as the pressures increased from 0.35 to 1.225 kg/cm^2. The somewhat higher percentage of survival of five pupae, to which pressures of 0.70 kg/cm^2 were applied in the latter test, as compared with the preliminary test, probably indicates protective irregularities in the surfaces of the blocks of clay with which the pressure was applied. The phenomenon probably also occurs in the field where irregularities in the soil offer a site in which less pressure is applied than on flatter surfaces.

The data from the field study (table 7) indicate that the pressures within the soil during a cultivation are great enough to cause some, but not major, mortality among pupating pink bollworms. The data confirm that the refuge along the top of the bed does not receive extensive pressure, but that the cutting action of the disk and the crushing together of blocks of dried soil may create localized areas of high pressure adequate to destroy the pupating pink bollworms. However, the majority would escape the pressures required to kill them. In the cultivated part, the pressures generally ranged from 0 to 0.70 kg/cm^2 except for the rows in which tractor tires ran. In rows through which the wheels do not pass, 30 to 60 percent of the pink bollworms would survive. The low recovery rate in the wheel rows (table 7) indicates that many of the capsules were driven into the soil by the tire lugs and mutilated beyond recognition. Therefore, few pupae would be expected to survive the passage of the wheels.

The destruction of fall crop residue and subsequent tillage to reduce overwintering populations of pink bollworms has been explored extensively (4, 7). However, the potential mortality through summer tillage has escaped the attention of most entomologists. The data presented here indicate that many pupating pink bollworms enjoy a refuge in the part of the row directly beneath the plants

8

Table 6.—*Mortality of pink bollworms after applying pressure to pupae between blocks of clay*

Pressure applied (kg/cm^2)	Number of replicates	Mortality range[1]	Mean[2]
		Percent	Percent
0	13	0-28	
.175	10	12-48	15
.35	9	24-64	32
.525	8	28-84	49
.70	8	56-88	63
.875	8	60-96	70
1.05	9	64-88	79
1.225	9	68-100	85

[1]Among number of replicates indicated.
[2]Corrected by Abbott's (1) formula for 13.5 percent mortality in the check replicates.

Table 7.—*Pressures within the soil caused by cultivation as indicated by pressure-sensitive capsules*

Capsule position	Percentage of original capsules recovered	Percentage of recovered capsules indicating kg/cm^2 of:				
		<0.35	0.35-0.70	0.71-1.05	1.06-1.40	>1.40
Adjacent to row:						
2 to 3 inches	80	50	50	0	0	0
3 to 4.5 inches	60	43	34	6	3	14
Shoulder of row	53	30	50	0	10	10
Side of row:						
With tire	27	0	14	0	14	72
Without tire	35	75	25	0	0	0
Bottom of row:						
With tire	6	0	0	0	0	100
Without tire	26	22	39	4	0	35

free from major mortality caused by normal field cultivations. The band of uncultivated soil provides an undisturbed, trashy, shaded, moist environment, which is an excellent survival site. Pink bollworms selecting pupation sites outside of this band are subject to burial and soil pressures that may result in a fairly high mortality under ideal circumstances. However, the survival rate is probably relatively high. Because the mature pink bollworm larvae dropping from the young, small plants will generally drop in the best available location in which to pupate, and the larvae tend to accept the first suitable pupation site they encounter, the uncultivated band beneath the row probably provides effective protection from many potential mortality factors and may be responsible for a high survival rate. As the plant canopy closes, resulting in cooler soil temperatures, cultivation ceases and more trash accumulates, creating more desirable pupation sites. The improved pupal survival contributes to larger, more damaging, late-season populations of pink bollworms.

LITERATURE CITED

(1) Abbott, W. S.
1925. A method of computing the effectiveness of an insecticide. Jour. Econ. Ent. 18: 265-267.

(2) Fye, R. E.
1971. Mortality of mature larvae of the pink bollworm caused by high soil temperatures. Jour. Econ. Ent. 64: 1568-1569.

(3) _____ and Bonham, C. D.
1970. Summer temperatures of the soil surface and their effect on survival of boll weevils in fallen cotton squares. Jour. Econ. Ent. 63: 1599-1602.

(4) Noble, L. W.
1969. Fifty years of research on the pink bollworm in the United States. U.S. Dept. of Agr. Agr. Handb. 357, 62 pp.

(5) Orphanides, G. M., Gonzalez, D., and Bartlett, B. R.
1971. Identification and evaluation of pink bollworm predators in southern California. Jour. Econ. Ent. 64: 421-424.

(6) Patana, R.
1969. Rearing cotton insects in the laboratory. U.S. Dept. Agr. Prod. Res. Rpt. 108, 6 pp.

(7) Watson, T. F., and Larsen, W. E.
1968. Effects of winter cultural practices on the pink bollworm in Arizona. Jour. Econ. Ent. 61: 1041-1044.

☆GPO 695-374